OPENING
Lotus Hawk's Prayers & Meditations

GUIDING PRAYERS FOR ANY DAY

Harriette "Lotus Hawk" Mandeville

ISBN: 978-1-4834-2214-5 (sc)
ISBN: 978-1-4834-2215-2 (hc)
ISBN: 978-1-4834-2213-8 (e)

Library of Congress Control Number: 2014920870

Lulu Publishing Services rev. date: 3/19/2015

Dear Cookie
Much Love
& Light
& Enjoy
Harriette

To my brother William, affectionately called Billy, who left this time and space as a young man but was really an old soul. Through my search for him I know he really never left me.

A prayer,
Just what would I say?
Speak of those who're around
Who pray for you every day

Everybody know we are just people
We are just people in the people's hands
Bless the soul of our man
That we might understand

Everybody knows we are just people
in the peoples hands
So keep a little prayer

—Excerpt from The Blind Boys of Alabama, "A Prayer"

ACKNOWLEDGMENTS

I am so thankful and grateful for the support of so many. Thanks to my husband Eddie, and children Billy and Dawn. Thanks to my computer guru, Lauren Eve and thanks to her sister, Jenna Rose for trying to teach me how to swim with words of meditation. Thanks to Susan for the first drafts of book and cover, and Jenny Vallon for her keen sense for the final edits, Kim Hughes, and Cynthia Maloney for their invaluable help. Thanks to Nina Sharma, and her mom, for the first readings.

Many thanks to my spiritual sisters "The Girls" who have been with me on my journey from Fisk, Sharon Davis, Kathy Ennix, Tena Gardner, Linda Gulley, Frances Rankin, and even more who through the years supported me and would not let me falter. Thanks to Jeree Wade, Ruth Hunt, Addie Little, Lynne White, Jonelle Procope, Cheryl Hill, Alicia Bythewood, Yolanda Brown, and to Caroline Jones who was one of my early mentors, who told me to write daily affirmations when we called them "thoughts for the day." Thanks to Reverend Denard for guidance and counsel. Thanks to Reverend Paul Smith for the "Big Rock" experience.

Thanks to everyone who has listened to any prayer or chant of mine and given me encouragement.

FOREWORD

The author strikes a delicate balance in providing information about the contemplative life of meditation and one's everyday activities. The meditations, prayers and affirmations are fresh and easy to use for those wanting to ground themselves in their daily rounds of life. The meditations are filled with the author's deep connection to the "spirit". That which grounds her is that which grounds the reader. She fulfills the seeker's need in the hunt for self-authenticity and one's hunger for the deep that lies within. The writer is what Howard Thurman refers to as "an apostle of sensitiveness" whose journey takes the reader to a place where one's spirit can be nurtured. The practices the writer speaks about are ones that have been a part of her daily routine. These creative writings are from her own experience with the Spirit and are easily acceptable to those in search of something meaningful in their lives. Finally these prayers and meditations address some of the deep insistent needs of the human spirit. They are needs that are universal and which all women and men may share. Their purpose is to focus the mind and heart upon the Creator as the Eternal Source and goal of life. So come center, reflect, meditate and be restored again as the author takes you on a spiritual journey.

Rev. Dr. Paul Smith

PREFACE

It still seems like yesterday. I am in the living room of our house, lying Camille-like on the chesterfield sofa. It's a hot and muggy summer evening, with a slight breeze. It's so quiet. The kids are at camp. Eddie is at a meeting. I am alone. The grandfather clock is ticking. I am listening dreamily to the sound. Eyes open and close.

I open my eyes, I close my eyes, I open my eyes, and I see a figure–a specter. I see this robed figure in my kitchen only for a few seconds, if that. It looks like the figure of a man in a monk's robe. The face is dark. Only the silhouette of someone. It feels like a vision of a religious figure. My stomach lurches as if I have been hit and it propels me up. "What was that? Who was that?" I get up. I move slowly to the kitchen. Still looking closely at the spot where I just saw this figure. I am barefoot. I walk warily on the parquet floors, about thirty feet, and then stop at the exact spot.

In the kitchen there is a window that looks onto the backyard. A typical Queens, New York backyard. The view is just of a straggly shrub-like tree, moving. The wind picks up just as I stare out the window. I continue to stare, then walk around, circling the spot, thinking maybe it will reappear. Maybe there is something that will prove what just happened. I look on the floor. I try to regroup and again stare out the window. "Was it just the tree moving outside?" I wish I wasn't alone. "It was just my imagination." I sigh and try to put those moments out of my head. "I didn't see anything, did I? It was just my imagination, right?"

Everyone I turned to had a different version of who or what they thought my vision was. I was asking everyone what they thought. What *I* was searching for was in the midst of all of *their* explanations.

Some time later I went to a meditation class with Rev. Danny Slaughter. He called it a spiritual development class. We would hold something of someone's and see what the energy read. Later I learned it was called psychometry. Then he would ask, "Does anyone have a question?" Of course I had a question. I wanted to know who that was in my kitchen. "That was how your brother came back to you. He is on a priestly level and he just wanted to show you himself so that you know he is okay. It required a lot of energy for him to clothe himself, but that was his message to you."

When I was twenty, my 19-year-old brother, Billy, was killed by a drunk driver. I had just married. He was in college. It was a shock to the system. That's when I first realized that we die. The church didn't prepare me for that and I grew angry with God.

Fifteen years later, he was the one in my kitchen. Only much later did I come to the realization that he was only supposed to be here for a certain amount of time. His time on Earth was over. My place was here, to be as creative as possible. I had to stop being angry with God because Billy was not totally taken away from me. He still existed in some sense. My journey was to find out where he was.

I didn't know it then, but that summer evening was the end of a gestation period of sorts. The death and apparition of my late brother sowed the seeds of spiritual awakening within me. It opened an avenue for me to explore *my* truth to lifes big questions. The search for my brother opened me to other ways I could connect with the Divine. This led to the birth of Lotus Hawk–an expansion of my identity into larger realms of perception, understanding and communication with the Divine. In other words, I am an intuitive.

My name is Harriette. About fifteen years ago when I was about forty-eight, I discovered the extension of my spiritual self and the name "Lotus Hawk" came to me. I smile when I think it's a name my mother didn't give me, but it's a name that has helped me reach my creative space. I know she won't mind.

The lotus flower is a symbol of awakening and is associated with rebirth. The lotus pushes itself through the mud of the earth to the light. It is symbolic of my search for rebirth and my constant reaching for spiritual light through my work.

The hawk is known in Native American cultures as a messenger, visionary and protector. The hawk reminds me of my brother and me rising higher and seeing with our "hawk eyes" messages and prayers to give you so you can live a life of sacred balance.

Words and names have energy. Sometimes people need something to draw them to someone who has a message. Even though Harriette and Lotus are the same person, the name Lotus Hawk has an energy that connects with people seeking what information I have to offer them. I need Lotus Hawk to be that beacon. In that way, it works better than Harriette Mandeville.

As an intuitive, I tune in to messages from the universe. More specifically, I tune into channels, or spiritual lines of communication, that transcend mortal existence. In other words my higher self has a conversation. The source of information is eternal–outside of time and space. There, everything that ever was and will be, just *is*. But because we are in time, we make up our messages about the past or future. For example, we can interpret them as a shared thought with someone far away, in the next room or someone who has passed. From the vantage point of the Source, it all just is. What you receive is just that–yours to receive, to be helpful with your journey.

These messages can come as a wide array of thoughts or feelings that don't seem to fit logically to the context they are presented in. Intuitively you know they are connected. We all experience it. It's like thinking of someone and then five minutes later the phone rings and it's the person you were thinking about! A channel connects you and that person in a higher realm. This is an example of our universal connection. Most people would call it a "coincidence." In a way, that is right. Two spiritual paths cross, or coincide. On our plane, they manifest as a thought and a call.

The messages are always there waiting for us to be open. When I began to study how people read energy, I learned that we all have this gift and if you want to use it, you can develop it. Tuning in is opening up, through conscious invitation, to receive whatever messages are yours among the many.

Opening is a collection of prayers, meditations, and affirmations, that began to arrive as I looked deeper into my gifts and into spirituality itself, unlocking a part of me I never knew existed.

TABLE OF CONTENTS

Part I
Seven Day Practice
1

Part II
Prayers and Meditations
27

Part III
Channeled Prayers
55

Part IV
Epilogue
61

PART I

SEVEN DAY PRACTICE

The intention of *Opening* is to give you a framework of daily spiritual practice aimed at opening you to the messages of the universe and to be in conversation and constant co-creation with God.

"The Artist's Way" by Julia Cameron was critical in my spiritual expansion and self-actualization. Her book is based on twelve weeks of writing. You just put the pen to the paper. You don't have to think about anything. You just write. What was really happening was a conversation with Spirit. It channels through to reach the paper, creating something useful.

According to Cameron, writing in the morning clears the cobwebs. If you have something you need to work through, either consciously or unconsciously, writing helps you get through it. It was amazing for me to look back on what I wrote. Many things had come to fruition years later. The prayers in this book came through this exercise. I tuned into a channel and, through me, messages came. Clear in my intention to serve, with practice and study, this process helped me on my journey to becoming Lotus Hawk–my highest creative self.

Be aware of the energy that created you, so you are able to operate at the level at which you were created. Becoming aware of God's energy moves us toward being our highest creative selves. In doing so we are able to reach out, help others, and be of service.

It is a good thing to meditate, relax the mind, and go into a quiet state. This is a moment of silence to acknowledge the Divine's omnipresent energy and give it "props." Visualize a silver cord that is connected to you and All-That-Is. Not simply connected to all things, but connected to the Creator of all things. The exchange of breath, in and out, keeps us connected with the Source, the Divine.

My process is intended to help you develop this discipline of daily practice. I hope that these four steps will help you overcome the blocks of the past and, at the same time, feel empowered to create the good that you want to manifest in your life.

LOTUS HAWK'S FOUR STEPS FOR SPIRITUAL READING

1. **Pray.** Place yourself in a comfortable position in a quiet spot. In the Seven-Day Practice read each prayer. Outside of that practice you may recite any prayer of your choosing or be in your own conversation with God. At its core, this step is the conscious initiation of conversation with the Divine.
2. **Meditate.** Again, be comfortable. Sit in a chair, with a straight spine, or lie down. Breathe. Become aware of your breath. Breathe through your nose, inhale slowly, pause, exhale slowly. Feel your lungs expanding and contracting.
   Focusing on the breath quiets the mind. Then listen and attune yourself to the still small voice. It may speak a word or phrase that resonates with you. Just sit. Sit with it so that it mixes with your thoughts, hopes, and dreams or what Howard Thurman would call an inward sea. Let it reach you at your deepest levels. In the practice, when quiet, we are listening, being still and opening a channel. It may not come at that moment. It may come later, at any time because you have cleared yourself.
3. **Write.** Meditation and writing go hand in hand. Like meditation, messages will not come from your mental chatter, but must burst through them. There is the action of your active mind in prayer and the meditation that stills the active mind. You have the positive habit of journaling daily. In this relaxed state, write without judging what is being created. This is listening to the inner voice. In my experience, my channel would tune in to a voice that represented the Mother Energy of the unconscious self. The words would just flow to my pen leaving their message as prayers
4. **Affirm.** Affirmations help you redirect your negative thoughts. For them to be effective they must be empowering, in the present tense, positive, personal, and specific.

Claim the circumstance as if it already exists:

I have everything I will ever need.
I am better every day, in every way.

Understand yourself as co-creator in your life. Take an active role in the creation of your life even though the circumstance may not be visible or even seem possible from your vantage point. You are constantly co-creating with the universe and by affirming you are actively using that power instead of passively floating, caught up in the currents of others, and even your own, negative beliefs.

The book is divided into four parts. The first is the guided seven-day practice that includes all four steps in my process including space for you to write what comes to you. Part II is a collection of prayers meant to add to your practice outside of Part I. They can be taken with you for guided conversation with God throughout the day. Part III consists of messages I have received throughout the years for you and the world. Finally, Part IV is a series of essays that came from spiritual musings.

FIRST PRACTICE

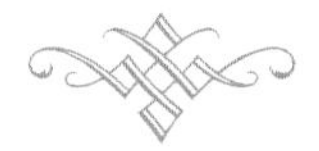

PRAYER OF AWARENESS

Today is a wonderful day
it's God's Day
it's a joyful day

Dear Lord,
For the awareness of my awakening
I give thanks.

For the awareness of my soul hearing your ever-present voice
I give thanks.

The awareness of your nearness
brings me peace.

Let my walking meditation
be the awareness that every step is taken
with Your light guiding the way.

✧ ✧ ✧

MEDITATION

Put yourself in the peace of the nearness of God. See a beautiful flower unfolding. See it blooming. It is awakening, slowly, balanced and aware of itself.

In your everyday reality, acknowledge that sometimes you don't notice your growth. You don't see it is all in good time. See that *your* flower is balanced in its blooming.

It may seem like things are not moving fast enough. But, look inside yourself to see that your life is directed to the right place at the right time. From a spiritual vantage point, without body, without ego, see yourself blooming.

Take a moment and meditate on what resonates in you from the reading of the First Practice. Practice breathing mindfully. Focus your awareness solely on the inhalation and exhalation of each breath.

AFFIRMATION

I see my way clearly.

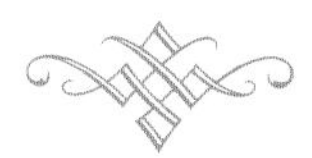

LIGHT OF THE SUN

I feel the glorious light of the rising sun
I pray to retain the awareness from where my power comes.

With the light of the Sun
I pray to be ever aware of Your power
that radiates from You
through me
around me
in me.

With the light of the sun
Help me to put away all that does not add good to my life
return it to the universe to be made into a loving energy again
to nourish my blessings.

With the light of the Sun
illuminate my awareness
to all that is.

Help me to know what they are
and in knowing
I can make peace with what they are
and let them go.

Help my soul radiate peace
burn with joy
glow with happiness
grow in harmony.

This day, as I breathe in and out,
I am open to my portion of good
from Your light.

✧ ✧ ✧

MEDITATION

Feel the nearness of God. Feel as though you are a bird flying with outspread wings, gliding against the backdrop of the rising sun. Ride the wind. Let majesty fill your center as you breathe in and out.

Take a moment to meditate on what speaks to you in a personal way. Continue to be in a quiet space, breathing the energy of Spirit in and then letting go of breath. Go with the flow.

AFFIRMATION

My breath connects me to my Source, God.
My breath connects me to peace and joy.

THIRD PRACTICE

PRAYER TO THE CREATOR OF THE UNIVERSE

Creator of the Universe,
Creator of my awareness that is
connected to You
I am the manifestation of your Divine Energy.

Help me connect and feel
the power of creation in myself,
the aura of the Creator around me.

Help me to harness
the loving power of the sun.

Give me the power to do unto others
as I would have them do unto me.

I pray to be strong
as the inner force moves me forward.

As I receive this awareness
I steady myself with Your loving power.

✧ ✧ ✧

MEDITATION

Feel the nearness of God. Feel gratitude as your spirit expands and melds with the Divine. Look inward and learn more about yourself and your power.

Your soul calls you to acknowledge your gifts. Work to use them without hesitation or fear. Acknowledge those obstacles and blocks, then leave them behind. Give thanks for today's message. Take it with you as you move through the day.

AFFIRMATION

I am centered and open for good to come my way.

FOURTH PRACTICE

PRAYER OF THE HEART

Dear Lord,
The Breath of Life
realign me.

Help me to wipe away the tears
to the beat of your will
trusting all is well.

Help me remove the discord of bitterness
forgive myself
forgive others.

Help me not judge myself
and not judge others.

Align me with the rhythm of love
keep me in the key of joy.

The loving Spirit fills me
with the universal beat.

As I listen
help me to know the sweet peace of
Your harmonious love.

✧ ✧ ✧

MEDITATION

Experience the nearness of God and presence of love. Feel the power of forgiveness in the loving heart of God. As you are, know you are in a space of love. Know your worry is solved. Your anger is absolved. Those who hurt you are forgiven. For not forgiving, you are forgiven. Walk today, knowing the rhythm of God moves you toward peace and joy.

Accept the light that shines on you with the message that all is well, all of the time. Adjust, and see this message is always there.

AFFIRMATION

Today I let go of resentments and let in love and harmony.

FIFTH PRACTICE

LISTENING PRAYER

Divine Spirit,

Give me strength
to hear Your holy, sacred voice
express Yourself in me
and through me.

I pray to be able to hear clearly
and accept Your will.

Help me hear the whisper of your will
discern my purpose and place
in the lofty peaks and deep valleys of life.

I pray to trust Your voice
receive Your message
without hesitation
and know today will be balanced and joyful.

✧ ✧ ✧

MEDITATION

As you are in a space of the nearness to the Divine. Feel the word of angelic voices whisper in your ear. Listen inwardly. Your soul may reveal the voices of angels encouraging you to move forward, get things done, fulfill your destiny, and not be afraid. Breathe in, out and quietly listen. Take this mindful practice with you throughout the day.

AFFIRMATION

I hear the voices of the angels and, today, I listen.
I am balanced and centered in all I do.

SIXTH PRACTICE

PRAYER TO ALL THAT IS

To All That Is
Was
and Ever Shall Be,

For expanding my world
Thank You
and growing every day in my connection to You.
Thank You

I pray that I am able to see Your visions
Know that we are not separate
and not doubt Your will.

I pray to appreciate everything created
to be open
and to trust
what I see coming from the Highest Spirit.

✧ ✧ ✧

MEDITATION

Feel the nearness of God. Be quiet, be in the moment. Picture the hustle and bustle of your day. Cars rushing by, the whirlwind of a busy street. What could the Divine be showing you? Take a few more breaths and continue to be in a mindful state. Take in the prayer while the visions become clearer. Sit in your moment of clarity.

This is a busy world we're in. Sometimes we get caught up in the whirlwind of life. As you continue the steps of spiritual reading, today's prayer will help you to center. When centered, you can discern what the best choices are for you. When centered, your confidence is anchored. You may be better able to express yourself to others and feel a connection to others by using your voice.

AFFIRMATION

I am a relaxed and loving spirit.

SEVENTH PRACTICE

PRAYER OF STILLNESS AND GRATITUDE

I take this moment to be still
I put my hands together
I and feel my breathing
I feel the universal breath of Inner Spirit.

I follow this channel
opened to the Great Spirit of many names.

I know this Source
is my protector and refuge.

I ask the Divine to hear my gratitude
for my blessings and awakening.

I pray to continue to know
that as I ask the universe
it creates the answers.

I pray that I continue to bathe in the mystery of life
and in its fullness and joy.

I ask You to continually bring light
and blessings to us on Earth.

Give me strength
to share this sacred space with all.

I now rest in knowing that all is well .

✧ ✧ ✧

MEDITATION

Feel the peace of the Divine. Settle in and feel assurance of the lessons that you have learned. Feel confident and centered in the present moment. Do this so you can walk with Spirit through your daily life, the life purposed for you by the Divine in order to have heaven on Earth, life as prescribed by the Golden Rule, life that makes you aware of your gifts and fosters the courage to use them.

AFFIRMATION

I am at ease and have no fear.

We ask you to continually bring light and blessings to use on Earth. And give us strength to share our sacred space with all. Rest in the knowledge that all is well.

Namaste and Amen

PART II

PRAYERS AND MEDITATIONS

I first thought that a seven-day practice would be sufficient. There are so many ways of describing being in a state of awareness. For instance, easily going to a place you find most peaceful and meeting your higher self or higher consciousness. Some of us describe it as being "in the zone." So, your state may just be a feeling of total peace. Total peace is certainly a positive state to be in during your daily life, wouldn't you agree? To be sure, this is one way that I have found to help me be more relaxed, definitely lowering my stress level and raising positive aspects of a joyful and balanced life.

Sometimes we just need to gird ourselves with positive words that will manifest the perfect guidance for us as we start our day. Each one of us starts our day differently. Up and out to work. Start the day getting the family ready to meet their day. Send the children off to school. Maneuver the morning chores. Take a moment to think of what is familiar to you. Say prayers for peace you can say at any time of the day. This is a peaceful state we would like to be in at all times. To some that might sound like a Pollyanna statement but not for me. If we exude this feeling then it transcends all. Lord knows, we need peace in the world. As you walk out of the door, say a prayer for peace. Write one down to keep with you when you feel stress. Or write your own. It is a good thing.

Prayers are a way of talking to God, and meditations are a way to listen. You can insert any name you like that represents your higher power. These prayers were written as I continued to open myself up to the belief that all our prayers can be answered and have seen how prayer and meditation moves us. You must remember to visualize your prayers as if they have already become a reality. Listen to your higher self speak as you relax, breathe, and open yourself to reach a place of balance and joy. Connect to your Source and hear the answers to your prayers. Then you can enjoy peace and understand the guidance that centers you and carries you through your days.

More examples of everyday prayers seemed to be a way to focus even more on the positive and stay in a state of openness and mindfulness. It gives more choices of prayerful words to read and accompanying affirmations to take with you during your day. Having more choices of daily prayers can give us a better chance of them becoming a positive habit. As these words are written, it matters only that the essence of the prayers be felt and disseminated. Only take in what feels right and good to you.

I am so happy to be able to share the peace and love of these words. Read them one by one. These prayers are not only for you but for all those around you. You can pick the prayer, affirmation, and meditation you need for the day. Pick one that family, friends, or the world may need. Maybe you will be guided to write your own prayers and speak your own words. Maybe you will receive affirmation that there is a higher power that loves you and is willing to listen to your prayers and answer them.

HELP

The prayer reminds me that our prayers are aways answered in times of need.

Dear Lord,

Help me be compassionate.

Help me not be fearful to use my gifts.

Help me use my gifts to help others.

Help me move to my highest potential.

Help me keep a smile on my face when all around me seems lost.

Help me have strength and courage to help myself.

Help me be able to help another navigate this day
this week,
and all the days that follow.

MEDITATION

Take a breath and ask, "What role am I choosing today?" Choose the part of someone who is self-confident and wears a loving smile.

Breathe in the moment your eyes open and you bound out of bed. Breathe out. Breathe in the knowledge that you will be the person that walks a successful path. Breathe out. See the sunshine spread to all around you, making all who cross your path smile

AFFIRMATIONS

I am in tune with the best things that this day brings. I put myself in the divine flow of the Spirit that is for my good.

WELLNESS

Dear Lord,

Let me see this day as a day of joy.

Let every soul feel Your radiant love.

Let me be reminded that all is well in Your eyes.

All is well in Your house so, all is well in mine.

✧ ✧ ✧

MEDITATION

As you breathe in and out think of God's creation and salute its beauty.

AFFIRMATION

Today I shine with God's light and healing.

DAY STAR

I greet the day star
shining star
with gratitude
and thankfulness.

I join in with the shining rays
and thank You for seeing the rising sun.

Grant me the strength today to meet any obstacles
give me courage to overcome them
accept the loving energy that fills me
share it with all around me
with my community, my family, and the universe.

MEDITATION

Breathe in the rays of the sun. Breathe out its light to all.

AFFIRMATION

I shine in my life, like the sun, every day.

TODAY

Today,
I pray to Spirit of my essence.

Spirit fill me with love and peace.

Watch my steps and protect me.

Protect me
essence of love
as I walk the day's journey.

I send you many thanks and much gratitude.

I accept your light and love for today's path.

✧ ✧ ✧

MEDITATION

Breathe in all that's good as you awaken for a new day.

AFFIRMATION

I am grateful. I fill myself with gratefulness.

TOMORROW

Dear Lord,
Bless me in your highest wisdom
to be in the now
as each day turns into tomorrow.

MEDITATION

Take on the role of a beautiful soaring bird, a visionary, a wise woman or man.

AFFIRMATIONS

I affirm that there are no obstacles I can't overcome in the days ahead.

PEACE I

The feeling and thoughts of peace connect me to the Divine.

Dearest Divine,
Send your guardian angels to remind me
that Your presence is already in me
and surrounding me.

Help me to know that the peace I wish for others
must start with me.

Help me to love myself
so that I know your peace.

Help me to hear your song of peace
that will heal my soul.

Help me to know that the peace of the world
starts with me.

MEDITATION

As you inhale love and exhale any chaos in your life, think of the songs of the morning birds bringing you music and thoughts of peace.

AFFIRMATION

Every day, I choose to put peace above all thoughts.
It is so, and so it is.
It is so, and so it is.
It is so, and so it is.
It is so, and so it is.

All is well
All is well [Ad infinitum].

PEACE II

Dearest Essence of Light,
The Highest Consciousness of the All-Good God
Help me to love myself
So that I know Your Love.

Help me to hear Your song of Peace clearly
So that I am in harmony with Your will.

Remind me, as I listen to my inner music,
that Peace is also God surrounding me.

Help me to know that the peace I wish for others
must start with me.

I know the song of peace
will heal my soul.

Peace is with me
Peace is me
Peace be with us all
Today, tomorrow, and always.

MEDITATION

As you inhale the golden light of love, feel it as warm as a comforting blanket. Exhale all the disturbances you feel in your life.

AFFIRMATION

I see peace everywhere I go I see peaceful trees, grass, flowers, water, birds and I see myself. I choose peace over all else.

PEACE III

Dearest Divine,
Thank you today for the energy of the sun
the energy from the ground
the energy from the sea
the energy from the air
the energy of sound.

I take it all in as I breathe,
acknowledging Your gifts to me.

As I see the totality of Your encompassing light,
I feel Your anchor in me
I feel Your loving Spirit caress me throughout the day
It brings peace to my being.

I pray that this awareness
not only continues in my space
but spreads to every one of my brothers and sisters.

I open my arms
raise them up with palms turned upward
to fully accept Your peace and grace.

I thank You for Your total love.

MEDITATION

Inhale the renewed exhilarating energy of your life. Feel its awe. Exhale any doubt you have about it.

AFFIRMATION

Today only the peace of the rays of sunlight and swaying trees in the wind grace my path. I accept all the good they bring.

PRAYER FOR THE CHILDREN

As I think of my inner child, I aways want the world's children to be safe.

Little ones
the wisest ones of all
I pray you grow strong
and remember your light at all times.

Pray fear never surrounds you or follows you.

I know angels are always watching over you.

I pray Spirit keeps you surrounded
with love, happiness and joy.

Thank you for the lessons you teach.

MEDITATION

Breathe in and breathe out. Connect with your inner child. You are in a place of success and safety. Breathe in creativity and courage. Breathe out fear.

AFFIRMATION

I am good at all I do. I am strong, smart, and safe. I affirm that my inner child expresses itself always and I know no fear. My creative, loving, and compassionate inner child keeps me in a safe and successful place.

PRAYER TO KNOW THYSELF

On the days that I struggle to understand my existence and who I am, a thoughtful prayer has put me on the right track.

Dear Essence of the Universe,
Please rain Your enlightenment down on me
That I may see my true self.

Help me see myself unadorned,
That I may receive Your will.

Help me see my arms open
to accept You as my shepherd.

Help me to have clarity
as I take my walk through life.

And know that my true self
is purposed to radiate Your Light.

✧ ✧ ✧

MEDITATION

Inhale, feel your inner Spirit and drop your clothed body. Exhale, and see your true self--think of yourself as a soul with a body.

AFFIRMATION

I affirm I know my true self. I am in a true place of clarity and light about myself.

PRAYER FOR COMPASSION AND UNIVERSAL LOVE

Sometimes I forget that what I think can affect the whole world. This prayer helps me look beyond myself and at what is really important.

Dear Spirit,
Help me today
to look beyond my human self.

Help me to connect
to the waves of energy that move in me
and through me.

Help me be grounded in
my connection to the world as one body.

Help me to understand
others I do not know.

Help me not judge
those I feel are on the wrong path.

Help me to feel
a loving energy for those I think are different from me.

Let me feel Your energy
that pulsates with every beat of my heart
and to act accordingly.

MEDITATION

As you inhale the loving breath of the earth feel a connection to everything. As you exhale, everything becomes clear and you are able to find and receive the good news.

AFFIRMATION

I am in a loving state at all times.

LIFE DAY | BIRTHDAY PRAYER

Each time that glorious day of our birth comes around, it is so good to give thanks.

Dear God,
Essence of my being
I rejoice today as I give a prayer of thanks to You.

Thanks for allowing me to have this glorious breath of life
to take in everything big and small.

I pray to continue this celebration of life
to see the tall leafy trees sway
to see the green grass grow under my feet
to see the creeping crawly ants on their daily march.

Ice cream, cake and candles,
hugs and kisses from the ones I love.

Thank You for bringing joy and happiness today
and many more life days to come.

MEDITATION

Breathe in the light of the candle. Breathe in the feeling of complete joy.

AFFIRMATION

This is a joyous day. All my days are joyous and full of love for myself and the universe.

PRAYER FOR THE BUSY PERSON

Sometimes we must stop to hear and see what is really important.

Oh, Dear God,
Please hear me.

Help me take a moment
to hear You.

Help me take a breath
and breathe in Your Light.

Not my everyday,
mundane
have-to-do
on-my-list
can't-stop
get-to-it-later
plate-is-full
thoughts.

Help me to take a moment in time
to stop
to open myself to Your light
to make sure my business
and where I am going
means something.

MEDITATION

Put your hands over your ears and close your eyes. As you inhale hear the sound of the ocean. As you exhale hear the waves of the ocean rocking you back and forth, returning you to your center.

AFFIRMATION

God's Spirit makes a way for all I need to be done.

SACRED BALANCE PRAYER

This prayer reminds me that I am always centered and that the universe only wants our perfect good.

Dear Mother-Father God,
hear my words,
so I may have strength to walk with You
so I may have courage to talk with You
so I may hear Your wisdom.

I pray You hear us as we speak to You.

I pray not to be fearful.

I pray to be open to receive Your knowledge.

Let me be able to be of service and help to others.

And as I am centered and hear Your words,
I know I will be able to feel Sacred Balance.

MEDITATION

Inhale and exhale. Think of the Sacred Balance for your mind, body and Spirit.

AFFIRMATION

Every day I have a balanced life. In every way I am aware of my goodness.

THANK YOU

Have you been awestruck by all the good things around you?
It feels good to say thank you.

As I breathe,
I am in a prayerful state.

I face the four directions of the universe
and I speak these words for us all:

I am thankful for all my blessings.

I am thankful for my perfect health.

I am thankful for all my good.

The Highest Spirit
Divine Energy
the Loving Source
always there for me,
bringing perfect harmony.

I am in the most positive place.

I thank God for guiding my way.

I am blessed.

I am healed.

MEDITATION

Breathe in and out knowing you are in perfect harmony.

AFFIRMATION

I affirm that this day and every day brings me all that is good. All is in perfect health and balance.

PRAYER FOR INNER GUIDANCE

Sometimes we just have to trust and remember our faith in "All That Is"

Dear Source of All That Is,
I pray for Your incredible and all-powerful light to let me see
you shining through this veil.

Let it dispel the darkness that I have let
be my illusion of days before.

I pray that You give me
the power to see Your goodness and love.

I pray to know
that it is already there for me to see.

Let me feel Your essence
Though you surround me and are in my whole being.

Let me see Your essence
though you are everywhere and I sometimes forget.

Remind me that I only need to look more deeply
to see Your essence more clearly.

Remind me to be still to hear Your voice.

I know You are in
and about us all.

When I am truly one with You,

I feel joy and Your indwelling
I feel harmony,
I feel balance,
I feel guidance.

I know You protect me and as I pray,
I see the light,
I am light and love, too

MEDITATION

Be still and sit quietly. Breathe in and out, follow the wind of your breath. Know you are firmly in the seat of the love of your Highest Source.

AFFIRMATION

I affirm:
I am
I see good
I feel I am guided this day
To all good things
I feel Your blessed hand
Resting on me
And so it is.

PART III

CHANNELED PRAYERS

There seems to be a consensus that there is a Divine Oneness that has created us. I believe there is a *single* Source. Due to the nature of its grandness, there is mystery. We pray to entities that go by different names. The avenues may seem separate, the sole purpose is the same–to get our messages to the Source. These are not only angels and saints. It includes Yoruba gods, Hindu deities, Native American totems and the like. I do not expect anyone to believe or disbelieve what I think moves this universe. Know that the words were written with the yearning to have each day start with prayer that would help ground my day with positive intentions.

Many communicate with this pulsating source that makes up "All That Is," our spiritual and physical world. We call this source of energy many names, God, the Father, the Mother, the Creator, etc. It is not important how we actually name it. It is just important that we feel its magnificence and are in conversation with it. In doing so, we delve deeper into what anchors our existence.

We forget that we are not in control. We have free will. We have choices. We have power. But we are not *the* Power. Sometimes we lose touch with awareness of the energy that is constantly around us, surging through and in us. We are not separate from the Energy. We are just a physical expression of it. We may not see it, but it's there.

The following prayers are to remind you that there are always spiritual beings that want to connect with us to help us.

FROM YOUR GUARDIAN ANGEL

These prayers are special to me because of the total loving energy of those visible and invisible who have helped me on my journey.

You are always a child to me
to be watched over
and kept safe.

It does not matter your mortal years.

You are a precious Spirit to be protected,
for however long you need Me.

Always, know that I am there.
Just raise your eyes upward to call on Me.

With a knowing nod
I will be there to guide you
In the name of light and love
the Divine Creator opens a way to you
So your guardian angel can always reach you.

FROM THE MOTHER EARTH

This is a prayer from the holy guards that reached me. This is a prayer for everyone.

Dear Child

Go to your Earth Mother,
she protects you.

She keeps you in her universal womb.

She frees you from all harm.

The words of prayers keep you strong
strong enough to take seed, grow,
and then nurture your own.

Have no fear for loved ones
big and small
far and wide
The blessed Energy keeps them safe.

Know you are watched over
we will not stray
there is plenty of love for you.

Open your arms
listen for the Voice
We are here.

All is well
you are full of grace.

Amen.

FROM THE MOTHER/GODDESS

Children of the Mother Goddess,
We pray with you as you move along the way.

We are watching over you
so you can call us for help.

Our names call out to you.

Know we are here.

Our voices come as melodies
deep within your soul.

Mother Mary calls to you
St. Therese calls to you
Green Tara calls to you
White Tara calls to you
Kuan Lin calls to you
Lakshmi calls to you
Grandmother calls to you

EPILOGUE

LIFE DANCE

As we walk through each day, we have concerns about our everyday life. Getting up, going to work, making money to support, feed, and do all the things we need to do to take care of our family. Not only our immediate family, but our extended families too. As well as making the time to spend time with our family and friends. It can truly seem as if this is a chaotic world and we have no control over it. Then once in a while, while this "life dance" is going on, we stop.

Why not stop for a moment and take stock of your day to day path from a different perspective? Try and really hear the music we are moving to more clearly. Ask yourself, what do you think keeps us moving, or "dancing" if you will, during our lives. However you call this energy, God, Divine Intelligence, a Higher Energy, The Source, a feeling of a Loving Essence. Whatever, your belief system calls this source of "All Things", the name is not important. Just the awareness of it keeps you in step with what is going on in your life.

When we stop and hear our beat, get our rhythm, snap our fingers, that allows us to get into a mellow groove or space. We all of sudden, understand what this dance we are doing is. We know we are the highest evolved beings in this universe, (we think we know anyway) and we know we are a part of something much, much bigger that can not all be explained. Some of which is still a mystery.

But we know we are living a day to day existence which is a wonderful thing. There is this glimpse of the beauty of it all. There are things around us, things that we see and sense. The beautiful plants, animals of every size and shape. Our family of man every size, color and disposition. Our galaxy that includes the sun, moon, and stars. Isn't it amazing that they appear right on time. When we take this moment to stop to hear the music, we are able to get a sense of how wonderful each individual being is.

And, as we allow it, an even greater sense overcomes us. A sense of connection to a greater being, our Spiritual Anchor. The energy, that keeps our spark of life lit while we are on this dance floor. Feel the magic and think of these steps.

1. Feel this connection through your breath.
2. Close your eyes and take a moment to inhale and exhale.
3. Recognize through your silent awareness, each part of your body relaxing.
4. Acknowledge invisible movements that pinpoint stress or some burden. Then let the thought go.
5. Be aware of the wisdom thoughts, knowledge, and (more) understanding of your life coming silently to you.
6. Now, feel a sense of being watched over by an energy of Love.
7. Take your time. Just for a moment or as long you like.

Now open your eyes. Know that we can always recreate that wonderful sense of peace. That wonderful sense of oneness with your Spiritual Anchor, a oneness that knows no separation. Let these thoughts lead you back to the dance floor. Back to moving to the music of life. Loving ourselves, one another, our community, our world. Trusting that we will be able to make the best choices. And, stay in step and energized by our highest "Musical Director".

Confidently knowing all is well and it's all fun and magical.

Namaste

February 12, 2012

My friend said to me, "that she belonged to the "School of Butterfly".

I instinctively knew, there was no actual school or edifice that she meant she had physically attended; that there was no registrar's office at this school that you physically went to sign up for your classes. But, it made me think, that as we move through life there are classes that we take that propel us to the next "grade". And, these classes have been evolutionary for my Spirit and moving to each grade has been quite fluid and continually going with the flow. Even though I know that life classes can get bumpy. It can just be the current of the wind taking you, the "butterfly" higher. It feels to me as we realize we are learning more about life we move on up and get our wings.

When I heard about the School of the Butterfly, I smiled. It made me realize we already belong. We are all a part of this universal school. The beautiful butterfly helps us to remember and be in the moment of balance and seeing clearly.

The butterfly that flutters in the wind, that dances on a petal as it moves towards the flowers scent and draws it near to drink the nectar. We see it in its full glory.

But, whence has she come, the egg, the larvae, the pupa, and finally the emergence of one more of God's creations.

We watch, we see the spirit of this creation.
We hear it whispering for us to listen and hear her teachings.
Teaching us to have patience.
To see beauty before it is fully manifested.
To see that there is a plan.
To see that life's struggles turn into growth.
And then finally see the triumphant creature, we name Butterfly.
We see it as it flutters in and out of our view.
Always in our mind's eye on the wind through the universe, graduate.

You ask, who belongs to the School of Butterfly?

You do, of course.

April 29, 2014

PEACE IN THE VALLEY

Peace in the valley is a term I often use when I want everyone to be happy in whatever situation they are in.

So, let's feel peace this morning. As we inhale and exhale, let's visualize beautiful scenery around us. Let us imagine we are in our hamlet below the mountain where there is a very old tree that draws us near because it has a spirit of a healing master. We sit next to our tree with our back being supported by our healing tree.

And now let us breathe in the air of our surroundings. We see in our panoramic view the beautiful, majestic mountains surrounding us. We are in a valley protected and safe. Let us continue to visualize this special place and continue our meditation

Breathe. Breathe. Breathe.

Let us inhale the nourishment of Spirit, God, the God Energy, Essence, however you name the source that surrounds us, and exhale joy and calm as we let go of our breath into the universe.

We feel our tree giving us strength as it stands tall. Feel the strength as it comes from the core of the earth, up through the roots through the soil of the earth that we are resting on. Feel its life giving force. Breathe.

We survey the mountains and the mountain tops, maybe they are even snow capped as we are snuggled safely in our valley of peace.

Breathe.

We are now conscious of being connected to the earth's energy. We are sitting at the seat of our healing tree receiving glorious rays of green filled rays from the earth's core, filling the body and soul, Don't fret, you only have to imagine it and it is.

Breathe.

Now see the rays streaming through the solid branches that stretch as far as the eye can see. Remember as you feel the warm golden rays energizing your Spirit, it is a celestial tree. The golden light streaming from high above the mountain tops, warming the body and soul.

Breathe.

As we inhale and exhale, affirm that "I am always filled with the life giving Light of the Universe" whether from above or below.
You are safe.
There is peace in the valley.

Namaste

November 22, 2013

SUGGESTED READING

Black Elk The Secret Ways of the Lakota by
Wallace Black Elk & William S. Lion
The Artist's Way: A Spiritual Path to Higher
Creativity by Julia Cameron
There is a Spiritual Solution to Every Problem by Wayne Dwyer
Creative Visualization Living in the Light by Shakti Gawain
Seth Speaks: The Eternal Validity of the Soul by Jane Roberts
The Way Toward Health by Jane Roberts
The Nature of Personal Reality by Jane Roberts
Science of the Mind by Ernest Holmes
The Tibetan Book of Living and Dying by Sogyal Rinpoche
You Can Heal Your Life by Louise Hay
Anatomy of the Spirit: 7 Stages of Power
and Healing by Caroline Myss
Edgar Cayce: An American Prophet by Sidney Kirkpatrick
The Seat of the Soul by Gary Zukav
Meditations of the Heart by Howard Thurman
The Encyclopedia of Symbols by Kevin Todeschi
Miracle of Mindfulness by Thich Nhat Hanh
Autobiography of a Yogi by Paramanhansa Yogananda

NOTES